Easy Password Tracker

Site	Username	Password

I0504018

Easy Password Tracker

Site	Username	Password

Easy Password Tracker

Site	Username	Password

Easy Password Tracker

Site	Username	Password

Easy Password Tracker

Site	Username	Password

Easy Password Tracker

Site	Username	Password

Easy Password Tracker

Site	Username	Password

Easy Password Tracker

Site	Username	Password

Easy Password Tracker

Site	Username	Password

Easy Password Tracker

Site	Username	Password

Easy Password Tracker

Site	Username	Password

Easy Password Tracker

Site	Username	Password

Easy Password Tracker

Site	Username	Password

Easy Password Tracker

Site	Username	Password

Easy Password Tracker

Site	Username	Password

Easy Password Tracker

Site	Username	Password

Easy Password Tracker

Site	Username	Password

Easy Password Tracker

Site	Username	Password

Easy Password Tracker

Site	Username	Password

Easy Password Tracker

Site	Username	Password

Easy Password Tracker

Site	Username	Password

Easy Password Tracker

Site	Username	Password

Easy Password Tracker

Site	Username	Password

Easy Password Tracker

Site	Username	Password

Easy Password Tracker

Site	Username	Password

Easy Password Tracker

Site	Username	Password

Easy Password Tracker

Site	Username	Password

Easy Password Tracker

Site	Username	Password

Easy Password Tracker

Site	Username	Password

Easy Password Tracker

Site	Username	Password

Easy Password Tracker

Site	Username	Password

Easy Password Tracker

Site	Username	Password

Easy Password Tracker

Site	Username	Password

Easy Password Tracker

Site	Username	Password

Easy Password Tracker

Site	Username	Password

Easy Password Tracker

Site	Username	Password

Easy Password Tracker

Site	Username	Password

Easy Password Tracker

Site	Username	Password

Easy Password Tracker

Site	Username	Password

Easy Password Tracker

Site	Username	Password

Easy Password Tracker

Site	Username	Password

Easy Password Tracker

Site	Username	Password

Easy Password Tracker

Site	Username	Password

Easy Password Tracker

Site	Username	Password

Easy Password Tracker

Site	Username	Password

Easy Password Tracker

Site	Username	Password

Easy Password Tracker

Site	Username	Password

Easy Password Tracker

Site	Username	Password

Easy Password Tracker

Site	Username	Password

Easy Password Tracker

Site	Username	Password

Easy Password Tracker

Site	Username	Password

Easy Password Tracker

Site	Username	Password

Easy Password Tracker

Site	Username	Password

Easy Password Tracker

Site	Username	Password

Easy Password Tracker

Site	Username	Password

Easy Password Tracker

Site	Username	Password

Easy Password Tracker

Site	Username	Password

Easy Password Tracker

Site	Username	Password

Easy Password Tracker

Site	Username	Password

Easy Password Tracker

Site	Username	Password

Easy Password Tracker

Site	Username	Password

Easy Password Tracker

Site	Username	Password

Easy Password Tracker

Site	Username	Password

Easy Password Tracker

Site	Username	Password

Easy Password Tracker

Site	Username	Password

Easy Password Tracker

Site	Username	Password

Easy Password Tracker

Site	Username	Password

Easy Password Tracker

Site	Username	Password

Easy Password Tracker

Site	Username	Password

Easy Password Tracker

Site	Username	Password

Easy Password Tracker

Site	Username	Password

Easy Password Tracker

Site	Username	Password

Easy Password Tracker

Site	Username	Password

Easy Password Tracker

Site	Username	Password

Easy Password Tracker

Site	Username	Password

Easy Password Tracker

Site	Username	Password

Easy Password Tracker

Site	Username	Password

Easy Password Tracker

Site	Username	Password

Easy Password Tracker

Site	Username	Password

Easy Password Tracker

Site	Username	Password

Easy Password Tracker

Site	Username	Password

Easy Password Tracker

Site	Username	Password

Easy Password Tracker

Site	Username	Password

Easy Password Tracker

Site	Username	Password

Easy Password Tracker

Site	Username	Password

Easy Password Tracker

Site	Username	Password

Easy Password Tracker

Site	Username	Password

Easy Password Tracker

Site	Username	Password

Easy Password Tracker

Site	Username	Password

Easy Password Tracker

Site	Username	Password

Easy Password Tracker

Site	Username	Password

Easy Password Tracker

Site	Username	Password

Easy Password Tracker

Site	Username	Password

Easy Password Tracker

Site	Username	Password

Easy Password Tracker

Site	Username	Password

Easy Password Tracker

Site	Username	Password

Easy Password Tracker

Site	Username	Password

Easy Password Tracker

Site	Username	Password

Easy Password Tracker

Site	Username	Password

Easy Password Tracker

Site	Username	Password

Easy Password Tracker

Site	Username	Password

Easy Password Tracker

Site	Username	Password

Easy Password Tracker

Site	Username	Password

Easy Password Tracker

Site	Username	Password

Easy Password Tracker

Site	Username	Password

Easy Password Tracker

Site	Username	Password

Easy Password Tracker

Site	Username	Password

Easy Password Tracker

Site	Username	Password

Easy Password Tracker

Site	Username	Password

Easy Password Tracker

Site	Username	Password

Easy Password Tracker

Site	Username	Password

Easy Password Tracker

Site	Username	Password

Easy Password Tracker

Site	Username	Password

Easy Password Tracker

Site	Username	Password

Easy Password Tracker

Site	Username	Password

Easy Password Tracker

Site	Username	Password

Easy Password Tracker

Site	Username	Password

Easy Password Tracker

Site	Username	Password

Easy Password Tracker

Site	Username	Password

Easy Password Tracker

Site	Username	Password

Easy Password Tracker

Site	Username	Password

Easy Password Tracker

Site	Username	Password

Easy Password Tracker

Site	Username	Password

Easy Password Tracker

Site	Username	Password

Easy Password Tracker

Site	Username	Password

Easy Password Tracker

Site	Username	Password

Easy Password Tracker

Site	Username	Password

Easy Password Tracker

Site	Username	Password

Easy Password Tracker

Site	Username	Password

Easy Password Tracker

Site	Username	Password

Easy Password Tracker

Site	Username	Password

Easy Password Tracker

Site	Username	Password

Easy Password Tracker

Site	Username	Password

Easy Password Tracker

Site	Username	Password

Easy Password Tracker

Site	Username	Password

Easy Password Tracker

Site	Username	Password

Easy Password Tracker

Site	Username	Password

Easy Password Tracker

Site	Username	Password

Easy Password Tracker

Site	Username	Password

Easy Password Tracker

Site	Username	Password

Easy Password Tracker

Site	Username	Password

Easy Password Tracker

Site	Username	Password

Easy Password Tracker

Site	Username	Password

Easy Password Tracker

Site	Username	Password

Easy Password Tracker

Site	Username	Password

Easy Password Tracker

Site	Username	Password

Easy Password Tracker

Site	Username	Password

Easy Password Tracker

Site	Username	Password

Easy Password Tracker

Site	Username	Password

Easy Password Tracker

Site	Username	Password

Easy Password Tracker

Site	Username	Password

Easy Password Tracker

Site	Username	Password

Easy Password Tracker

Site	Username	Password

Easy Password Tracker

Site	Username	Password

Easy Password Tracker

Site	Username	Password

Easy Password Tracker

Site	Username	Password

Easy Password Tracker

Site	Username	Password

Easy Password Tracker

Site	Username	Password

Easy Password Tracker

Site	Username	Password

Easy Password Tracker

Site	Username	Password

Easy Password Tracker

Site	Username	Password

Easy Password Tracker

Site	Username	Password

Easy Password Tracker

Site	Username	Password

Easy Password Tracker

Site	Username	Password

Easy Password Tracker

Site	Username	Password

Easy Password Tracker

Site	Username	Password

Easy Password Tracker

Site	Username	Password

Easy Password Tracker

Site	Username	Password

Easy Password Tracker

Site	Username	Password

Easy Password Tracker

Site	Username	Password

Easy Password Tracker

Site	Username	Password

Easy Password Tracker

Site	Username	Password

Easy Password Tracker

Site	Username	Password

Easy Password Tracker

Site	Username	Password

Easy Password Tracker

Site	Username	Password

Easy Password Tracker

Site	Username	Password

Easy Password Tracker

Site	Username	Password

Easy Password Tracker

Site	Username	Password

Easy Password Tracker

Site	Username	Password

Easy Password Tracker

Site	Username	Password

Easy Password Tracker

Site	Username	Password

Easy Password Tracker

Site	Username	Password

Easy Password Tracker

Site	Username	Password

Easy Password Tracker

Site	Username	Password

Easy Password Tracker

Site	Username	Password

Easy Password Tracker

Site	Username	Password

Easy Password Tracker

Site	Username	Password

Easy Password Tracker

Site	Username	Password

Easy Password Tracker

Site	Username	Password

Easy Password Tracker

Site	Username	Password

Easy Password Tracker

Site	Username	Password

Easy Password Tracker

Site	Username	Password

Easy Password Tracker

Site	Username	Password

Easy Password Tracker

Site	Username	Password

Easy Password Tracker

Site	Username	Password

Easy Password Tracker

Site	Username	Password

Easy Password Tracker

Site	Username	Password

Easy Password Tracker

Site	Username	Password

Easy Password Tracker

Site	Username	Password

Easy Password Tracker

Site	Username	Password

www.ingramcontent.com/pod-product-compliance
Lightning Source LLC
Chambersburg PA
CBHW070541220526
45467CB00003B/1016
9781706883371